Contents

Kitchen Know-How 4

A Giving Christmas: a Note
  to Children 5

The Gift of Christmas 6

BASIC RECIPES:

Sweet Dough 10

Gingerbread Dough 12

Savory Dough 14

Claydough 15

Playdough 16

Royal Icing 17

Water Icing 17

MAKING AND BAKING ACTIVITIES:

Savory Stars 18

Icing Snowflakes 20

Strings of Stars 22

Popcorn Garlands 23

Table Place Names 24

Star Candleholders 26

Star Candles 27

Stained-Glass Window Cookies 28

Hearts on Hangers 30

Tic-Tac-Toe 32

Napkin Rings 34

Refrigerator Magnets 36

Tree Ornaments 38

Doves of Peace 40

Christmas Cards 42

Star Card Hanger 44

Door Wreath 46

A Note to Adults 48

KITCHEN KNOW·HOW

Here are a few handy hints to make your cooking time a fun time. First of all, remember to ask if you may use the kitchen. Make sure that a grownup is around in case something goes wrong. Then remember these simple rules for happy cooking.

◆ Wash your hands and wear an apron or old shirt.

◆ Tie back long hair.

◆ Keep the work surface clean and clear.

◆ Mop up spills at once—wet floors are dangerous.

◆ Always use oven gloves when carrying hot things and put them on a heat-resistant surface.

◆ Be careful with knives—never hold the blade, and always cut downwards on a chopping board.

◆ Check that electric appliances are off before plugging them in. NEVER touch electric sockets with wet hands.

◆ If you can't reach something, ask a grownup to help.

◆ Read through the recipe before you start. Get all the ingredients and utensils ready. Follow the recipe step by step. Sometimes recipes include unfamiliar words, for example, a teaspoon is written as "tsp" and a tablespoon as "tbsp".

◆ To stop dough from sticking when you roll it out, first sprinkle a little flour on the work surface and the rolling pin.

◆ Have fun cooking and leave the kitchen tidy—then you will always be welcome to use it again.

A Giving Christmas

Christmas is all about loving and giving—so here is a book of fun presents for you to make or bake, and give to your family and friends. If you're running out of ideas for interesting and inexpensive Christmas decorations and gifts which you can make yourself, this will give you fresh inspiration.

Any grownup will tell you that there is something very special about gifts made by children. They're special because they mean that you care enough to take time away from all the things that interest you to make something for someone else. When you spend time making something special for someone, in a way you are giving a little bit of yourself, and so your gift becomes a gift of love.

That's really what Christmas is all about— showing people we care about them. We celebrate Christmas because God sent his gift of love, a baby called Jesus, to show us that he cares for us. What a wonderful reason to celebrate!

The Gift of Christmas

The Emperor Augustus couldn't have chosen a worse time for a census. Poor Mary was due to have her baby any day and here she was, perched uncomfortably on the back of a donkey, making the long journey south from her home town Nazareth to Bethlehem. There she and Joseph, her husband, were to register and pay their taxes.

It was a relief to the weary pair to see the welcoming lights of Bethlehem. They soon found that the town was crowded with fellow travelers all coming to register, and every bed was taken. At inn after inn they were told there was no room for them, but at last a friendly innkeeper took pity on Mary.

"I can see your baby is due very soon," he said. "You're welcome to share with the animals. There's plenty of room. It's not as comfortable as the inn, but it is warm and dry and the straw is clean."

Mary and Joseph accepted gratefully, relieved to have somewhere to sleep.

Later that evening, in the stable alongside the animals, Mary's baby son was born. She wrapped him tightly in cloth and Joseph filled a manger with clean straw to serve as a crib. They named their child Jesus.

As Mary and Joseph looked proudly

down at their baby boy, they talked in hushed voices about the amazing events that had led to this night.

Joseph was a carpenter, and he and Mary had planned to be married. Mary had busied herself with preparations for their life together. One day, a strange and wonderful thing happened. An angel called Gabriel appeared to Mary. Terrified, Mary could only stand and stare.

"Do not be afraid, Mary," he said. "You have found favor with God."

Then he told her that she had been chosen by God to bear a very special baby, a child who would become a king greater than any other the world had seen. She was to name him Jesus, the Son of God.

Scarcely able to speak with fright,

Mary had whispered, "I am the hand-maiden of the Lord, be it as you say."

Now, here in front of her lay that baby—the fulfilment of the promise made to her by the angel Gabriel.

The quiet didn't last long. Suddenly, into the stable burst a breathless group of shepherds.

"Where is the baby king?" they asked. "Is it true? Have we come to the right place?"

"Yes, you have," said Joseph in amazement. "But how did you know?"

They all started talking at once, jabbering excitedly.

"Hold on, hold on! One at a time," begged Joseph.

They told him that earlier that night they had been looking after their sheep

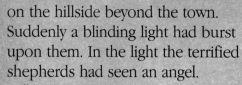

on the hillside beyond the town. Suddenly a blinding light had burst upon them. In the light the terrified shepherds had seen an angel.

"Fear not—I bring great news. Today, in the city of Bethlehem, a Savior, Christ the Lord, is born. You will find him wrapped in cloth and lying in a manger."

All around them the sky had filled with angels singing, "Glory to God in the highest and on earth peace, good-will to all people."

Just as suddenly as they had come, the angels disappeared, leaving the shepherds again in the dark night wondering if they had been dreaming.

But no, it hadn't been a dream, for here indeed was the child—in a man-ger just as the angel had promised.

The shepherds were so excited that on their way back to tend their sheep, they stopped everyone they met and told them of the wonderful things they had seen that night.

Far, far away something just as wonderful was happening. For years, a group of wise and wealthy scholars had scanned the sky, watching, waiting for the star that would signal the com-ing of a great king. And there it was! A brilliant light in the night sky, making all the other stars pale by comparison.

"Hurry! Pack our bags and make ready the camels," they said to their servants. "We must leave at once and follow the star."

For many weeks they traveled, always at night with the star as their guide. At last they came to Judea and the palace of Herod, a cruel and fearsome king. "Herod will know where to find the child. Let's go and ask him," they decided.

Herod hadn't heard anything of this baby and was very angry at the thought of another king in his land. Fearful for his throne, he hatched a plan. Pretending to be glad to hear the wise men's news, he asked them to come back and tell him when they had found the baby. "I would like to worship him too," he told them, but secretly he plotted to kill the baby.

Anxious to find the king, the wise men journeyed on, following the star until it stopped above a house in Bethlehem, bathing the building in light.

Mary and Joseph were amazed when they saw their visitors. Before them stood the wise men, their rich embroidered cloaks and jeweled turbans glinting in the starlight. Mary and Joseph were a bit awed and not too sure what to do. Should they bow?

But no, it was the wise men, these rich and powerful Magi who bowed and knelt down before the baby sleeping in his mother's arms. From their packs they took the most precious things they possessed—fine gifts of gold, frankincense and myrrh—and laid them in front of the baby.

Mary smiled and looked down on the Christ Child. She knew in her heart that in in her arms lay the most precious gift of all—God's gift of love to the world. And that is the real gift of Christmas that we celebrate each year.

These dough recipes may be used with many of the Christmas activities given later in this book. But they don't need to be kept just for Christmas—you can use them at any time of year. There are recipes to make sweet or savory biscuits, gingerbread people, or claydough models and decorations, using designs of your own.

Sweet Dough

✶ ✶ ✶ ✶ ✶ ✶ ✶ ✶ ✶ ✶ ✶

This basic sweet dough can be used for a variety of cookies. (If you are using the dough with a recipe later in this book, you need to follow the instructions only as far as step 6.)

YOU WILL NEED

- ◆ 1 cup plain flour
- ◆ ¹/₂ cup margarine or butter
- ◆ ¹/₃ cup sugar
- ◆ 1tsp grated lemon rind
- ◆ 1 small egg
- ◆ large mixing bowl
- ◆ small mixing bowl
- ◆ teaspoon
- ◆ knife
- ◆ wooden spoon

- ◆ fork
- ◆ rolling pin
- ◆ foodwrap
- ◆ baking tray, greased
- ◆ wire rack

BASIC RECIPES

1 Set the oven to 350° F.

2 Use the large mixing bowl. Cut the margarine or butter into small cubes, add the flour and the grated lemon rind.

3 Using your fingertips, rub the flour and margarine or butter together until the mixture looks like breadcrumbs.

4 Add the sugar.

5 Beat the egg in the small mixing bowl with the fork. Add the beaten egg to the mixture in the large bowl. Mix with the spoon and then knead until you have a smooth, firm ball of dough.

6 Place in foodwrap or a plastic bag and put in the refrigerator for 20 minutes.

7 Roll out to $1/8$ in. thick on a lightly floured surface. Then cut out using your chosen shapes.

8 Bake for 8–10 minutes until golden brown.

9 Cool on a wire rack.

B A S I C   R E C I P E S

✕ ✕ ✕ ✕ ✕ ✕ ✕ ✕ ✕ ✕ ✕ ✕

Gingerbread dough is made in a pan on top of the stove, so be sure that you can reach it comfortably and safely. This dough can be used with cutters to make both gingerbread people and little cookies. (If you are using the dough with a recipe later in this book, you need to follow the instructions only as far as step 7.)

YOU WILL NEED

◆ 3/4 cup brown sugar

◆ 3/4 cup light corn syrup

◆ 1tsp cinnamon

◆ 1tsp ground ginger

◆ 1tsp ground cloves

◆ 6oz (1 1/2 sticks) butter

◆ 1 egg

◆ 1tsp baking soda

◆ 1tsp cold water

◆ 3 1/4 cups plain flour

◆ large heavy-bottomed pan

◆ wooden spoon

◆ 2 tablespoons

◆ teaspoons

◆ fork

◆ 2 small cups or mixing bowls

◆ rolling pin

◆ baking tray, greased

◆ wire rack

1 Set the oven to 350°F.

2 Put the sugar, syrup, spices and butter into the pan and stir gently over a low heat, until the butter has melted.

3 Turn off the heat and remove the pan from the cooker. While you wait for the mixture to cool, beat the egg in a cup or mixing bowl with a fork. Dissolve the baking soda in the water in another cup.

4 Add the egg to the pan, and stir.

5 Stir the baking soda into the mixture—it will fizz and bubble.

6 Add the flour, one spoon at a time, mixing well with the wooden spoon. It will get more difficult towards the end but you should end up with a glossy dough.

7 Put the dough in the refrigerator to cool for 20 minutes.

8 Roll the dough out on a lightly floured surface to $1/8$ in. thick. Then cut out using your chosen shapes.

9 Place on a baking tray and bake for 8–10 minutes.

10 Cool on a wire rack.

BASIC RECIPES

S a v o r y   D o u g h

This dough can be used to make little savory cookies. (If you are using the dough with a recipe later in this book, you need to follow the instructions only as far as step 6.)

YOU WILL NEED

◆ 1 cup plain flour

◆ 2oz (¹/₂ stick) margarine or butter

◆ 1 cup finely grated cheddar cheese

◆ ¹/₂ tsp salt

◆ 1tsp dry mustard

◆ ¹/₂ tsp paprika

◆ 1tsp dried mixed herbs (optional)

◆ 4tbs water (approx.)

◆ large mixing bowl

◆ teaspoon

◆ tablespoon

◆ foodwrap

◆ rolling pin

◆ baking tray

◆ fork

◆ wire rack

1 Set the oven to 350°F.

2 Cut the margarine or butter into small squares and add to the flour in the large mixing bowl.

3 Add the mustard, salt and paprika.

4 Add the herbs—if you don't like the idea of green bits in your cookies, leave them out!

5 Using fingertips, rub the flour and margarine or butter together until you have a crumbly mixture. Add the cheese. Slowly add the water, one spoon at a time. Keep kneading the mixture until a smooth, firm ball of dough is formed. Add a little more water if necessary.

6 Place in foodwrap and put in the refrigerator for 20 minutes.

7 Roll out on a lightly floured surface to 1/8 in. thick. Cut out cookies using your chosen shapes.

8 Put on greased baking tray and bake for 10–12 minutes until golden brown.

9 Cool on a wire rack.

This is definitely not for eating but is wonderful for making crafts and decorations. You need a bit of patience as it takes several hours to harden. It makes a good alternative to modeling clay from a craft shop.

YOU WILL NEED

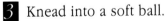

◆ 1 3/4 cups plain white flour

◆ 2tbsp salt

◆ 1/2 cup cold water

◆ large mixing bowl

◆ wooden spoon

◆ tablespoon

◆ measuring cup

◆ plastic bag

1 Put the flour and salt in a large bowl.

2 Slowly add the water, mixing thoroughly.

3 Knead into a soft ball.

4 Use right away or keep in an airtight container or plastic bag.

BASIC RECIPES

Playdough

Homemade playdough is very easy to make and will keep for quite a long time. It is very useful for keeping young children busy while you are busy with your own crafts. Remember this is only for play, not for eating.

YOU WILL NEED

- ◆ 1³/₄ cups plain white flour
- ◆ 1¹/₄ cups salt
- ◆ 3tsp cream of tartar
- ◆ 2tbsp cooking oil
- ◆ food coloring
- ◆ 1 cup water
- ◆ saucepan
- ◆ teaspoon
- ◆ tablespoon
- ◆ measuring cup
- ◆ wooden spoon
- ◆ plastic bag or airtight container

1 Put all the dry ingredients into the saucepan.

2 Add the oil and the food coloring.

3 Gradually add the water and stir with the wooden spoon over a low heat until it thickens.

4 Let the dough cool and then knead until it forms a soft lump.

5 Store in an airtight container when not in use.

Royal Icing

This icing is excellent for making Christmas tree decorations such as the *Icing Snowflakes* on page 20. When left to dry it goes rock hard.

YOU WILL NEED

- ◆ 2 egg whites
- ◆ 3 cups powdered sugar
- ◆ 1tsp cream of tartar
- ◆ food coloring (optional)
- ◆ large mixing bowl
- ◆ sieve
- ◆ teaspoon
- ◆ wooden spoon

1 Sieve the powdered sugar into a large mixing bowl.

2 Add the cream of tartar.

3 Separate the eggs (you need only the egg whites). Ask for help if you haven't done this before. Lightly whisk the egg whites to soft peaks, then add to the powdered sugar.

4 Mix thoroughly using a wooden spoon. The icing should be very stiff.

Water Icing

This icing is suitable for decorating homemade cookies.

YOU WILL NEED

- ◆ 1¹/₂ cups powdered sugar
- ◆ 2tbsp cold water
- ◆ food coloring (optional)
- ◆ mixing bowl
- ◆ sieve
- ◆ wooden spoon
- ◆ teaspoon
- ◆ tablespoon

1 Sieve the powdered sugar into the mixing bowl.

2 Add the water and mix well—make sure that there are no lumps.

3 Add a drop of food coloring if you want colored icing. The icing is now ready to use and should be soft but not runny.

BASIC RECIPES

Savory Stars

★ ★ ★ ★ ★ ★ ★ ★ ★ ★ ★

Homemade snacks and "nibbles" are always popular at Christmas. Warm these savory stars in the oven before serving.

YOU WILL NEED

◆ one batch of savory dough (see page 14)

◆ rolling pin

◆ flour (for rolling out)

◆ star-shaped cookie cutter

◆ baking tray

◆ fork

◆ wire rack

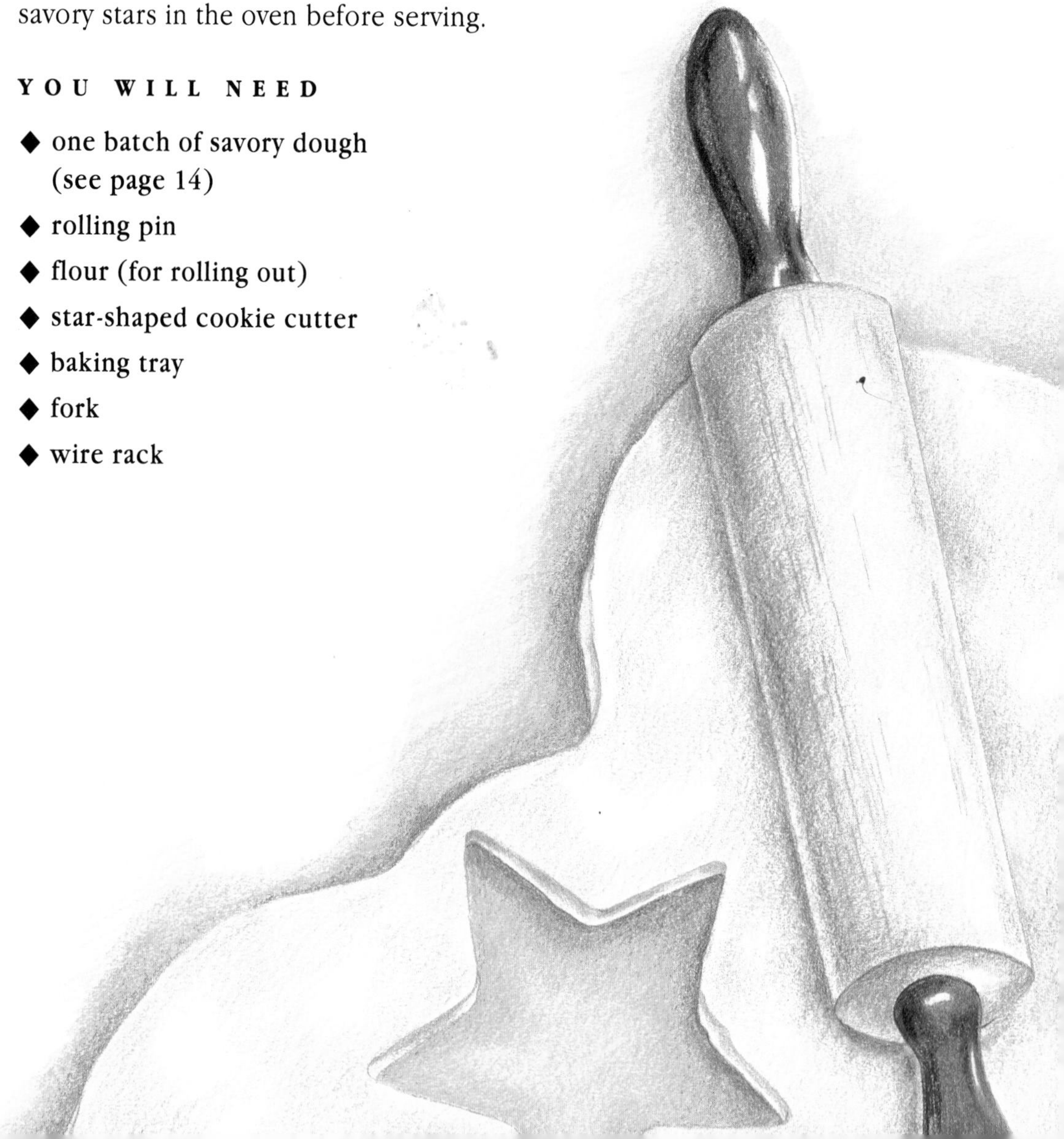

1 Set the oven to 350° F.

2 Make the savory dough.

3 While the dough cools, grease the baking tray.

4 Roll out the dough on a lightly floured surface to about $1/8$ in. thick.

5 Cut out star-shaped cookies and space evenly on the baking tray.

6 Gently make a pattern with the fork on the stars.

7 Knead and roll left-over dough for more stars.

8 Bake for 10–12 minutes.

9 Cool on a wire rack, then store in an airtight container.

Icing Snowflakes

These Christmas tree decorations
need a couple of days to dry. They are
rather delicate but they look very pretty.
Younger children will need help to
make them.

YOU WILL NEED

◆ royal icing (see page 17)
◆ icing bag and plain icing nozzle
  (medium hole)
◆ sheet of waxed paper
◆ pencil and tape
◆ nylon thread or narrow ribbon
  (gold, silver or white are ideal)

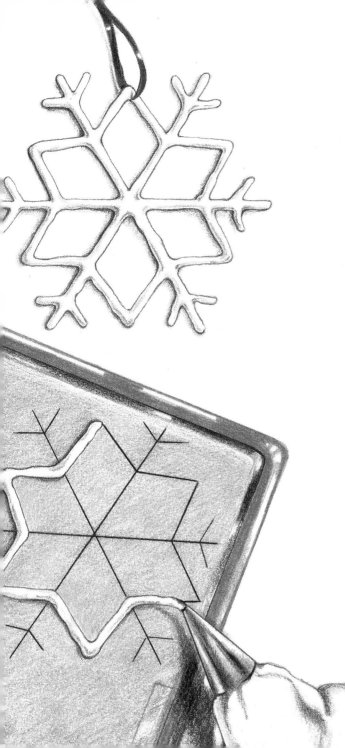

1 Trace the snowflake outline on the left 6 or 7 times onto the waxed paper. (Leave spaces between the shapes.)

2 Put the waxed paper on a flat baking tray. Use tape on the edges to stop it slipping.

3 Using the icing bag, carefully ice over the outlines.

4 Leave to harden for 2 to 3 days.

5 When completely dry lift the snowflakes carefully off the paper. Use a palette knife or spatula.

6 Loop the nylon thread or ribbon through each snowflake and hang them on the tree.

Icing snowflakes also make good Christmas cake decorations. A base of pale pink or pale green icing with white snowflakes on top would be very pretty.

Some of the simplest Christmas decorations are often the best. Even a very young child can make these.

YOU WILL NEED

◆ a packet of gold or silver gummed stars
◆ dark green or black thread

1 Simply stick two stars together back to back with the thread running between them, and then do the same with more pairs of stars. Space them at $1^1/_2$ in. intervals, leaving enough thread at each end to make a loop for hanging on the tree.

2 For variety you could make a double star by mismatching them when you stick them together.

P o p c o r n   G a r l a n d s

★ ★ ★ ★ ★ ★ ★ ★ ★ ★ ★ ★

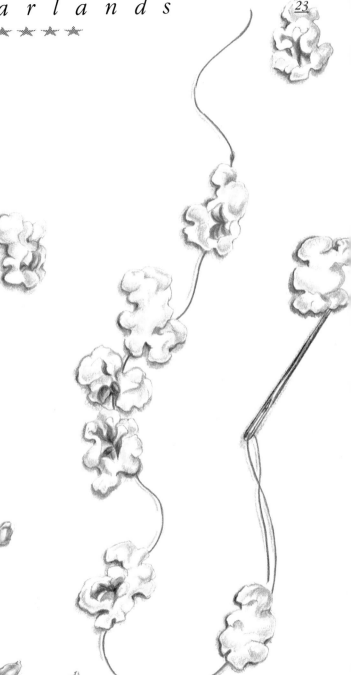

These tree decorations are a favorite with many children. The difficult part is resisting the temptation to eat them before they get to the tree!

YOU WILL NEED

◆ large bowl of cooked popcorn. Use either one bag of microwave popcorn or 4oz popcorn kernels. Cook according to the instructions on the packet.

◆ darning needle and thread. Use a piece of thread about 2 yards long

Tie a knot at one end of the thread. "Sew" through a piece of popcorn, pushing it right up to the knot. Continue to "sew" the rest of the popcorn, piece by piece, to make a garland. Use several of these instead of tinsel on your Christmas tree.

Table Place Names

✦✦✦✦✦✦✦✦✦✦✦✦

Place names add a personal touch to a table setting and are helpful when there are a number of guests.

YOU WILL NEED

- ◆ one batch of claydough (see page 15)
- ◆ cookie cutters
- ◆ rolling pin
- ◆ baking tray
- ◆ small knife
- ◆ glue
- ◆ enamel paint, poster paint or felt-tip pens, and clear varnish
- ◆ paint brushes
- ◆ gold or silver pens
- ◆ glitter or sequins (optional)

1 Set the oven to 100°F.

2 Make claydough and roll out on a lightly floured surface to about $1/8$ in. thick.

3 Choose shapes for the place names— hearts or stars look good. Cut out the number of shapes you need.

4 With a knife cut out the same number of A-shaped triangles measuring $1 1/4$ in. x $1 1/4$ in. x 1in.

5 Place on the baking tray and bake for 3 hours. You can leave overnight until completely hard and dry.

6 Paint the shapes and triangles.

7 When the paint is dry, write the guests' names on the shapes with a felt-tip pen.

8 Put a line of glue down the center of the back of each shape and along one of the long edges of each triangle.

9 Stick the shape to the triangle.

10 If you have used poster paint or felt-tip pens, seal with a coat of varnish once the paint is dry.

11 If you wish, glue on sequins, or dip the edges in glue and then in glitter.

Once these candleholders are painted, nobody would guess that they are made from flour and water! Two of these in a pretty box will make a super gift.

YOU WILL NEED

◆ one batch of claydough (see page 15)

◆ rolling pin

◆ baking tray

◆ star-shaped cookie cutter

◆ cold water

◆ ruler

◆ small knife

◆ sandpaper or emery board

◆ enamel paint, or poster paint or felt-tip pens and clear varnish

◆ paint brushes

1 Set oven to 100°F.

2 Make claydough. Roll out the dough on a lightly floured surface to about 1/4 in. thick.

3 Cut out 6–8 star shapes.

4 Gather up spare dough and roll out again.

5 Using a knife, cut 6–8 strips 3/4 in. wide by 2 1/2 in. long.

6 Moisten the center of the star and one long edge of the strip with a little water. Bend the strip into a circle and stick it upright on the star to make the holder.

7 Gently place on a baking tray and bake at 100°F for 4–5 hours or leave overnight in an oven on low heat.

8 Take the candleholders out of the oven and leave to cool. Meanwhile, cover the work surface with newspaper. Gently smooth off any rough edges with sandpaper or an emery board.

9 Now have fun painting the candleholders. Remember to paint inside and underneath.

10 If you have used poster paint or felt-tip pens, seal with a coat of varnish once the paint is dry.

11 For extra sparkle, glue on beads or sequins.

✳ ✳ ✳ ✳ ✳ ✳ ✳ ✳ ✳ ✳ ✳

This is a very simple but effective way of making ordinary candles Christmassy.

YOU WILL NEED

◆ candles—any size or color. If you have made the star candleholders on the opposite page you could make matching candles

◆ a packet of gold or silver gummed stars

◆ gold or silver ribbon

Simply stick the stars around the candle, evenly spaced but not too near the top. A pair of navy blue candles decorated with gold stars and tied together with a gold ribbon would make a lovely Christmas gift.

Stained-Glass Window Cookies

★ ★ ★ ★ ★ ★ ★ ★ ★ ★ ★ ★ ★

These unusual Christmas cookies use the sweet dough recipe. Each tree-shaped cookie has a beautiful transparent center, just like a stained-glass window, and makes an attractive Christmas tree decoration.

YOU WILL NEED

- ◆ one batch of sweet dough (see page 10)
- ◆ 16–18 clear hard candies in assorted colors
- ◆ rolling pin
- ◆ cups or small mixing bowls
- ◆ teaspoon
- ◆ small plastic bag
- ◆ sheet of waxed paper
- ◆ small knife
- ◆ tree-shaped cookie cutter
- ◆ baking tray
- ◆ drinking straw
- ◆ narrow ribbon, yarn or thread

1 Set the oven to 350° F.

2 Make sweet dough and put in refrigerator to cool for 20 minutes.

3 Cut the waxed paper to fit the baking tray.

4 Using one color at a time, put the hard candies in the plastic bag and crush them with a rolling pin. Put them aside (do not mix the colors) in cups or small mixing bowls.

5 Sprinkle flour on a flat surface and on the rolling pin, then roll out the dough to about 1/8 in. thick.

6 Using the cookie cutter, make the tree shapes and place on the waxed paper.

7 Using the knife cut out a triangle at the center of each cookie—leave a good edge at the top.

8 Fill each triangle with crushed hard candy, using only one color for each cookie. Be generous.

9 Use the drinking straw to make a hole at the top of the tree-cookie so you can thread a ribbon through it later.

10 Bake for 8–10 minutes until golden brown.

11 While the cookies are still warm, check that the hanging holes are clear. If not, gently make them again.

12 Leave on the baking tray until cold—this is very important because the candy "windows" need to harden.

13 Gently lift the cookies off the paper and store them in an airtight container until needed.

14 Thread yarn or ribbon through the holes, make loops and hang on the Christmas tree. They don't keep for very long, but you probably won't find that a problem!

Here are some more edible Christmas
tree decorations made out of gingerbread dough. You can, of course, use
shapes other than hearts if you like.

YOU WILL NEED

◆ gingerbread dough (see page 12)

◆ water icing (see page 17)

◆ heart-shaped cookie cutter

◆ fine, colored ribbon or yarn—
approximately 2 yards

◆ assorted edible cake decorations—
silver balls, chocolate chips,
sprinkles, etc.

◆ icing bag and plain nozzle

◆ small knife

◆ drinking straw

◆ rolling pin

◆ baking tray, greased

◆ wire rack

1 Set the oven to 350°F.

2 Make gingerbread dough.

3 When cool, roll out to about $1/8$ in. thick.

4 Cut out heart shapes using the cookie cutter.

5 Take half the cookies and make a hole at the top of each one with a drinking straw (so that you will be able to hang it up).

6 Take the other cookies and cut a circle out of the center of each one.

7 Bake on a greased baking tray for about 8 minutes until golden brown.

8 If the hanging holes have closed up in the baking, gently make them again while the cookies are still warm.

9 Cool on a wire rack.

10 While the cookies are cooling, prepare the icing and fill the piping bag. Now set your imagination free—decorate with icing squiggles and patterns, stripes, dots, names, anything you like. Or simply ice and add silver balls, chocolate chips or sprinkles.

11 Allow the icing to dry. Cut the ribbon or yarn into 6in. lengths and loop them through the cookies. Hang on the Christmas tree or keep in an airtight container until needed.

Tic - Tac - Toe

This is a popular game for two players that both children and grown-ups can enjoy. Making your own game is fun. Wrap it in a pretty box and you have a lovely gift.

YOU WILL NEED

◆ one batch of claydough (see page 15)

◆ sharp knife

◆ baking tray

◆ rolling pin

◆ white card

◆ pencil and ruler

◆ 2 colors of enamel paint, or poster paint or felt-tip pens and varnish

◆ paint brushes

◆ small round cookie cutter or small glass

1 Set the oven to 100°F.

2 Make the claydough.

3 Roll out on a lightly floured flat surface to about 1/4 in. thick.

4 Cut out 5 circles using the small round cutter or glass.

5 Cut out 5 squares 11/4 in. x 11/4 in.

6 Using the sharp knife cut a hole in the center of each circle.

7 Cut sections of the squares away to form X's.

8 Put on a baking tray and bake for 2–3 hours.

9 Paint each piece, making the 0's one color and the X's another. Make sure you cover all the surfaces with paint. If you have used poster paints or felt-tip pens, seal with varnish when the color is dry.

10 Mark up a piece of white card 6in. x 6in. with a grid as shown. Each player choses one shape and takes turns to place their chosen shape on the grid. See who is first to complete a matching row.

Napkin Rings

These napkin rings give a festive look to the Christmas table.

YOU WILL NEED

◆ colored card in a number of colors
◆ for shapes use various cookie cutters
◆ glue
◆ scissors
◆ ruler
◆ pencil and felt-tip pens or gold and silver pens
◆ braid or beads for decoration

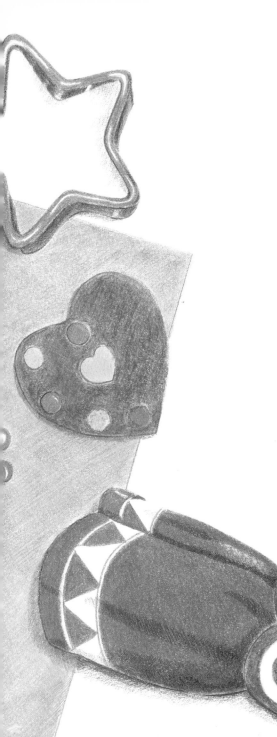

1 Using the ruler, measure and mark rectangular strips of card $1^{1}/_{4}$ in. x 6in. Cut these out.

2 Glue the ends of each strip together to form a ring and leave to dry.

3 Using the cookie cutters as templates trace the shapes onto a card of another color. Cut out these shapes.

4 Decorate each shape—using felt-tip pens, gold and silver pens, glitter, beads or braid—and perhaps add a name.

5 Glue the shape onto the ring—over the line where you joined the edges.

Refrigerator Magnets

These are easy to make and useful too. They make fun presents, and you might like to wrap one in a little parcel to put into someone's Christmas stocking.

YOU WILL NEED

◆ one batch of claydough (see page 15)

◆ 5 or 6 small magnets (from craft shops or hardware stores)

◆ strong glue

◆ small knife

◆ water

◆ enamel paint, or poster paints and clear varnish

◆ paint brushes

◆ felt-tip pens

◆ assorted cookie cutters

◆ baking tray

◆ rolling pin

1 Set the oven to 100°F.

2 Make the claydough and roll out on a lightly floured surface to 1/4 in. thick.

3 Press out shapes with the cookie cutters or make your own shapes with a knife. How about a face, a flower or a snowman? (To make a snowman use bits of dough to add the eyes, nose, hat and scarf. Stick them on with a little water.)

4 Carefully put the shapes on a baking tray and bake for 3–4 hours or leave overnight in a warm oven.

5 Paint when completely hard and dry. If you use poster paint or felt-tip pens, seal later with varnish.

6 When the paint is dry, glue the magnet onto the back of the shape.

Christmas Tree Ornaments

★ ★ ★ ★ ★ ★ ★ ★ ★ ★ ★ ★ ★

Homemade decorations are much more special than bought ones. Children of any age can make these.

YOU WILL NEED

◆ one batch of claydough (see page 15)

◆ small knife

◆ drinking straw

◆ cookie cutters in Christmas shapes

◆ baking tray

◆ rolling pin

◆ enamel paint, or poster paint or felt-tip pens and varnish

◆ paint brushes

◆ narrow ribbon or thread

1 Set the oven to 100° F.

2 Make the claydough. Roll it out on a lightly floured surface to 1/4 in. thick.

3 Cut out shapes with cutters, or make your own shapes using the knife.

4 If you want to stick pieces onto the shapes, for example a star on a tree or a little heart in the center of a bigger one, moisten the surfaces with a little water and they will stick.

5 Use the straw to press out a hole at the top of each decoration by which to hang it.

6 Carefully put the shapes on a baking tray and bake for 3–4 hours until hard.

7 Some ideas for painting the shapes: try using one color on one side and a different color on the other. Or try stripes, dots or fluorescent paint. Don't forget to paint all the surfaces. If you are using poster paint or felt-tip pens, seal later with varnish. Leave to dry.

8 Pull the ribbon or thread through the holes and tie to form a loop. Now hang your decorations on the tree.

D o v e s   o f   P e a c e

Hang these gentle white doves on your Christmas tree as symbols of peace.

YOU WILL NEED

◆ a sheet of tracing paper

◆ a sheet of lightweight card or stiff paper

◆ a sheet of white tissue paper

◆ a pencil or pen

◆ an eraser

◆ a ruler

◆ a darning needle and thread

◆ a pair of scissors

1 Using tracing paper, copy the outline of the dove (see below) onto a piece of card. Very carefully, mark the slit for the wings and the position of the hole for the hanging thread. Cut and use this as a pattern to trace onto the sheet of card as many doves as you need.

2 Use the white tissue for the wings. Measure and cut out a rectangle measuring 4in. x 3³/₄ in. for each dove. Using your ruler and pencil, mark points at ¹/₃ in. along the long edges.

3 Fold, accordion style, at each of the pencil marks until you have a strip resembling a closed fan. Fold this strip exactly in half.

4 Mark the eyes on the body of the dove.

5 Cut a slit for the wings on the body of the dove as marked.

6 Slide the folded fan through this slit and check that the wings are centered and evenly balanced. Gently spread the fan of the wings.

7 Using the darning needle, pull a loop of thread through the hole as marked. Again it is important to be exact so that the dove hangs correctly.

You could try using patterned tissue or a lacy doily for the wings.

Christmas Cards

★ ★ ★ ★ ★ ★ ★ ★ ★ ★ ★ ★

Homemade Christmas cards add that
extra personal touch. And it is much less
expensive to make your own!

YOU WILL NEED

◆ a sheet of plain card

◆ a sheet of colored cellophane or
tissue paper

◆ envelopes

◆ pencil, crayons or felt-tip pens

◆ scissors

◆ glue

◆ cookie cutters

◆ braid, sequins, glitter for decoration

Cut and fold the plain card to sizes that will fit inside the envelopes.

2 Using a cutter as a stencil, draw its outline on the front of the card.

3 Carefully cut out the shape.

4 Cut a piece of cellophane or tissue paper the same size as the folded card front.

5 Glue this inside the front of the card to give a stained-glass window effect.

6 Decorate the front of the card either by drawing or with glitter, sequins, gummed stars or braid.

7 Write your message inside with a felt-tip pen—gold would look pretty.

Star Card-Hanger

★ ★ ★ ★ ★ ★ ★ ★ ★ ★ ★

Keeping Christmas cards tidy is a problem for many people. This hanger will be a welcome gift.

YOU WILL NEED

◆ stiff gold or silver card
◆ pencil and ruler
◆ pins
◆ scissors
◆ glue
◆ star-shaped cookie cutter
◆ 1 yard of wide ribbon (cheaper from florists)
◆ thread

Using the cookie cutter and the pencil, trace a star onto a piece of scrap paper.

2 Enlarge the star by adding 3/4 in. all around. Use your ruler.

3 Cut out the star to use as a stencil.

4 Now put the stencil on the metallic card, draw around it and cut out a star.

5 Glue the ribbon to the back of the star, so that it hangs down.

6 Make a loop from the thread and glue it to the back of the star. Now you can hang the star up.

7 Put the pins at regular intervals along the length of the ribbon. Cut a "V" out at the end of the ribbon to finish it off.

Door Wreath

This is a traditional decoration which you can make out of claydough. You will probably need to ask a grown up to help you put this together, but even young children can easily make the shapes needed.

YOU WILL NEED

◆ a double batch of claydough (see page 15)

◆ small knife

◆ enamel paint, or poster paint or felt-tip pens and varnish

◆ paint brushes

◆ baking tray (extra large)

◆ a broad ribbon, $1/2$ yard long

◆ picture wire

1 Set the oven to 100° F.

2 Make a thick "snake" from one batch of dough, about 1in. thick and 18in. long.

3 Flatten the "snake" with your hands and join the ends to make a circle. Use a little water to stick the ends together.

4 Roll out the second batch and cut out some shapes. To make a holly wreath, cut out different-sized holly leaves and arrange them, slightly overlapping, on the circle. Stick each leaf to the circle with a little water.

5 Roll "berries" from the left-over dough and stick them on between the leaves.

6 Leave space at the top for a big bow.

7 Gently put on the large baking sheet and bake overnight.

8 Make sure the wreath is properly dry before painting. It is important to seal all surfaces (front and back) either with enamel paint, or varnish on top of poster paint or felt-tip colors.

9 To finish, tie a large bow at the top of the wreath. Make a loop from picture wire and tie securely around the top of the wreath so that you can hang it on the door.

You could try other less traditional themes. Dark blue and gold stars would be striking. A dove of peace would be unusual. The possibilities are endless!

A NOTE TO ADULTS

This book is a collection of fun activities to help children celebrate the Christmas season and to keep them busy over the holidays. Depending on their ages, they will need some help with getting everything together, supervision in using appliances and, of course, plenty of encouragement and praise—however misshapen or lop-sided the outcome!

But this is not just an activity book. It is also about gifts and giving. These days, it is easy for both children and adults to be caught up in the pressure at Christmas time to spend and "get." Yet, for many, all the consumerism reminds us that we and our children have lost something of the real spirit and significance of Christmas.

Giving and being thankful are at the heart of the Christmas message. This book gives an opportunity to talk to your children about caring, giving and sharing. You can encourage them to consider God's message of love at Christmas and to think of people less fortunate than themselves. You may be surprised at how easy this is—children have a remarkable innate spirituality and capacity to love. If you are able to help them glimpse the true meaning of Christmas, you will be giving them a priceless gift.